Padre

CW00819974

REV. JUDE WINKLER, OFM Conv.

Imprimi Potest: Michael Kolodziej, OFM Conv., Minister Provincial of St. Anthony of Padua Province (USA)
Nihil Obstat: Rev. James M. Cafone, M.A., S.T.D., Censor Librorum
Imprimatur: ✠ Most Rev. John J. Myers, D.D., J.C.D., Archbishop of Newark

The Nihil Obstat and Imprimatur are official declarations that a book or pamphlet is free of doctrinal or moral error. No implication is contained therein that those who have granted the Nihil Obstat and Imprimatur agree with the contents, opinions or statements expressed.

Printed in China   ISBN 978-0-89942-531-3   CPSIA   March 2015   10 9 8 7 6 5 4 3 2 1   L/P

Padre Pio as a Boy

PADRE Pio was born on May 25, 1887, in the small village of Pietrelcina in the south of Italy. His parents, Grazio and Giuseppa Forgione, were poor and honest farmers. They owned a few pieces of land on which they raised grapes, wheat, corn, olives, figs and plums, almost all of the food that their family needed to survive.

Grazio and Giuseppa named their son Francesco (which in English is Francis). He was not known as Pio until he became a Franciscan.

Francesco was a good little boy. He loved to pray in church, especially when he could be there alone. He also hated to hear swearing, which was very common in the area where he was growing up. Whenever he heard someone swearing, either he would make a Sign of the Cross and say his prayers or he would rush away.

One day he saw a Capuchin Franciscan, Friar Camillo, passing by. The Capuchins are followers of St. Francis of Assisi, and they dedicate themselves in a special way to poverty and prayer. Friar Camillo was gathering the offerings of the people to help support the friars. Little Francesco decided that he wanted to join the "friars with a beard" (for in those days all Capuchins wore beards).

Francesco Grows Up

FRANCESCO would not have an opportunity to enter the Capuchins for several years. In the meantime he would have to learn his lessons. The family wondered where they would find the money to pay his tutors. They had enough to eat, but very little cash. So Grazio, Francesco's father, traveled first to Brazil and then to the United States to earn money for his son's education.

The boy was not a great student, but he learned enough to keep progressing. His greatest difficulty was his delicate health, something from which he suffered most of his life. There were times, in fact, when his family despaired for his life, but he would eventually recover.

Then, when Francesco was fifteen years old, he entered the novitiate of the Capuchins. This is the first year of religious life in which one learns the traditions and the spirit of one's order. It is a time of prayer and discernment (figuring out whether God has called one to this type of life).

Upon entering the novitiate, Francesco received the name he would use for the rest of his life, Pio (which is Pius in English).

Friar Pio Grows in Holiness

IN his early years in the order, Friar Pio traveled from friary to friary, learning the lessons he needed to be a Capuchin friar and eventually a priest. Those who knew him in these early days spoke of how pleasant it was to live with him. He was an example of obedience and humility. They missed him whenever he was away, and that was quite often. His illness continued to bother him terribly in those days.

It was during his early days in the order that the friars began to notice his extraordinary spiritual gifts. He would have periods of time when he saw and spoke with Jesus, the Angels and the Saints. This is called an ecstasy.

It was around this time that he is also said to have received the gift of bilocation (the ability to be in two places at one time). While he was in his friary, he appeared to a man who was dying very far away. The man was an enemy of the Faith, and Friar Pio convinced him to seek God's forgiveness. That very night the man's wife gave birth to a daughter to whom Padre Pio became a spiritual advisor years later. Padre Pio knew her even before they had been introduced (for he was present when she was born).

Padre Pio as a Young Priest

ON August 10, 1910, Friar Pio was ordained a priest. From then on he would be known as Padre Pio. On the holy card that was printed for that day, he wrote that he wanted to be "a holy priest, a perfect victim." From his earliest days as a friar and a priest, he offered himself up to God as a victim. He wanted to suffer for his own sins and the sins of others so that they might turn to God.

At first Padre Pio's suffering involved physical illnesses. For a number of years, he would enter one of the order's friaries and immediately become so ill that he would have to be sent home. It was at this time that he first received the stigmata, the wounds in his hands, feet and side that Jesus had on the Cross. The stigmata was not yet permanent, for it would appear and then fade away.

In 1915 Italy entered the fighting of World War I. The government drafted priests and friars into the army, where they often served in the medical corps. Padre Pio was called to his medical exam, which he failed, but the government drafted him anyway. Yet, almost as soon as he arrived in his barracks, he became so violently ill that he was sent home to recover.

Padre Pio as Spiritual Guide

BEFORE and after he was drafted, Padre Pio lived in a town called San Giovanni Rotondo. He would live there for the rest of his life.

He quickly acquired a reputation for holiness among the people in that region. Many people went to him for spiritual advice. He would often know more about them than they were willing to tell him. He received this knowledge directly from God.

Padre Pio would give direction only to those about whom God had given him information. He did not want to direct them on his own, for he felt that this would be an act of pride. He wanted to obey God in all things.

There were five rules that Padre Pio suggested for spiritual growth. He told people that they should go to confession once a week. They should receive Holy Communion every day. They should read spiritual books on a regular basis. They should meditate upon God and the truths of our Faith. Finally, they should examine their consciences daily so that they could become aware of the ways in which they were growing and find those areas in which they still needed work.

It was around this time that he began the first prayer groups that eventually spread worldwide.

Padre Pio Receives the Stigmata

ON August 5, 1918, Padre Pio received the gift of the stigmata. He was to carry these wounds for the next fifty years.

Many Church officials and doctors examined his wounds. Some of them thought that he might be faking his wounds, but, after examining him, almost all were convinced that his stigmata was truly from God.

Padre Pio would especially suffer while he was celebrating the Holy Mass each day. It was as if he were experiencing just what Jesus did on the Cross. Like Jesus, he would lose much blood from his wounds. He always offered up these sufferings for the salvation of the world.

Word of Padre Pio's stigmata spread throughout the town and the region. Many people had become terribly discouraged by the war, and they needed the consolation of knowing that God was still working in their midst. Many people confessed their sins to him, firmly believing that this was an encounter with God's mercy.

Every once in a while there was a rumor that Padre Pio was going to be transferred from San Giovanni. The people of that village would hold meetings and march to his convent to make sure that no one would take their beloved friar from them.

Padre Pio Obeys
His Church Superiors

A ROUND this time some Church officials began to question whether Padre Pio was truly saintly or not. Part of the problem was that there were people who seemed to have been jealous of him. They even made up lies, saying that he was not faithful to his vows.

Another part of the problem was that people who were loyal to Padre Pio were not always nice and gentle. They would push and shove to get a better spot in the chapel where he celebrated Mass and listened to confessions. There were even people selling clothes that were covered with blood from animals that they claimed were relics of Padre Pio.

For these and other reasons, the Church placed some rules upon how Padre Pio could do his ministry. Twice he was ordered to do things that would limit his contacts with people outside of the friary. For example, he was to say Mass at a different time every day so that the people would not know when to expect him.

It was during these periods that Padre Pio proved his holiness most. He humbly obeyed whatever orders he was given, even if some of these things made him sad. He always wanted to fulfill God's will as expressed through his superiors.

Padre Pio's Fame Grows

AS word of Padre Pio's stigmata and holiness spread throughout the region and all Italy, and then eventually over the whole world, he received more and more requests for prayers. It took a number of friars to answer these letters and to promise those requesting prayers that Padre Pio would remember them in his own prayers.

In those days, there was a young American woman from New Jersey named Mary Pyle who became a disciple of Padre Pio. She was quite rich, and she built a large house in San Giovanni. There she could host visitors to Padre Pio. She helped his ministry in whatever way she could until the day she died.

Padre Pio heard the confessions of many people. Those who were sincere found him to be understanding and gentle. But Padre Pio was harsh with those who just wanted to go to confession to a famous priest. He often sent them away until they were truly sorry for their sins. Then he would welcome them warmly, for he knew that they were ready to change their lives.

There were even a number of people who either belonged to other religions or did not believe in God at all who became Catholics as a result of meeting Padre Pio. They could sense that God was working through him.

Padre Pio, Example of a Humble Life of Service

MANY people began to make offerings of money to Padre Pio. At first, these were most welcome, for his friary was very poor and could use the money just to buy food and clothes for the friars. But as more and more money arrived, Padre Pio began to use it to help poor families. Some of them had visited or written to him, asking for his help; others did not even have to contact him. He had been informed by God that this or that family was in need, and he would send money to help them.

There was never a question of Padre Pio using the money for his own comfort. Everyone agrees that he lived a humble, simple lifestyle.

Padre Pio ate very little. He would join the other friars whenever they had meals, but he would hardly touch his food. No one could understand how he could survive. It was as if God was nourishing him with His love.

It also seemed as if he hardly ever slept. He would sleep only around three hours each night. His other time during the day was spent in prayer and meditation and serving God's people, especially by listening to their confessions and offering spiritual advice.

Padre Pio Battles the Evil One

IT is said that the holier one becomes, the more the devil bothers you. Padre Pio was bothered by terrible temptation, even by visits from the devil, for most of his life. The devil would try to trick him and make him do things that would not have pleased God.

Padre Pio was truly courageous in this battle. He would always make sure that his messages came from God by asking those who appeared to him to praise God and glorify Jesus. If they refused, Padre Pio would know that the messenger did not come from God.

He would also rely upon the protection of his Guardian Angel and the other Angels. He often told people who visited him in San Giovanni that they should go to a shrine not far from there that was dedicated to St. Michael. He is the Archangel who forced Satan out of heaven. Padre Pio told his visitors that St. Michael would protect them from the action of the devil.

But Padre Pio's greatest weapon against the devil was to dedicate himself to God's love more and more. Later in his life, he told people that he did not believe that there could be many people in hell because God was so merciful and loving.

World War II Arrives

IN 1939 World War II began in Europe. Italy became an ally of Germany and was fighting in Europe and Africa. At first the battles went well for Italy, but that did not fool Padre Pio. He predicted that it would go very badly for Italy and that she and her allies would lose the war. He felt that the leader of Germany, Adolf Hitler, was a very evil man and that Italy should never have become his friend.

In 1943 the war had gone so badly for Italy that many Italian cities were being bombed by American and English airplanes. San Giovanni was not a very large city, but it was still almost bombed a number of times.

Something very unusual happened whenever the bombers approached San Giovanni. The pilots spoke of seeing a bearded friar dressed in a brown robe, who stood in front of their planes. Sometimes the friar was normal in size, but other times he was enormous. Later, when these airmen visited San Giovanni, they would recognize the friar as Padre Pio.

Once the Americans landed in southern Italy, they began to make trips to San Giovanni to visit Padre Pio. Many of the soldiers who had been lazy and disobedient before their visit turned their lives around after their meeting with Padre Pio.

The House to Relieve Suffering

EVEN though Padre Pio suffered from illnesses all throughout his life, he did not like to see others suffer. This is why he had a small hospital built that was named St. Francis Hospital.

In 1938 the hospital was destroyed in an earthquake. Padre Pio decided that he would replace the hospital with a much larger building that would be called the "House to Relieve Suffering." Padre Pio provided the first donation, a coin that was worth only a few pennies. The coin had been given by a very poor woman who gave Padre Pio all that she had so that he might rebuild the damaged hospital.

Because of World War II and all the problems that it created, it took many years for Padre Pio and his helpers to collect the money needed to finish this project. The house finally opened in May of 1956.

Padre Pio hoped that the house would be a place where those recovering could receive both physical and spiritual assistance. He had been in hospitals during World War I, where staff took care of only the body but never showed the patients the love and prayer that they truly needed. This is why Padre Pio insisted that the House to Relieve Suffering not be called a hospital; it was to be so much more than that.

"God Will Provide"

AS Padre Pio began his project, he chose the doctor who would organize the construction of the House to Relieve Suffering. The doctor had not really believed in God when he first met Padre Pio. His whole life turned around when he met him and he became a good Christian.

Padre Pio told the doctor that he would have to be in charge of the project. The doctor answered that he could not do it because he had to earn a living for his family, a difficult task to do in San Giovanni. But Padre Pio told the doctor, "God will provide."

Upon returning to his home city of Florence, the doctor won the lottery. He was able to sell everything he had in Florence and move to San Giovanni, where he first designed and then supervised the construction of the House to Relieve Suffering.

In 1949 an even greater miracle was bestowed on a man named Giovanni Savino. On February 12, Padre Pio told him to be courageous because he would not die from what was about to happen. Then, three days later, he was seriously injured by an explosion on the job. He lost his right eye completely. But several days later the man said that Padre Pio had visited him. When the man's bandages were removed, the doctors discovered that his right eye had grown back.

Padre Pio Grows Old

BY the end of the 1950s and the beginning of the 1960s, Padre Pio had grown quite old. He had the normal aches and pains that one develops as one grows older, but he also suffered from the serious illnesses that plagued him all of his life.

In May of 1958, he grew sicker and sicker. He was so ill that he was not even able to listen to confessions or celebrate Mass. Some doctors even thought that he might be dying of cancer, but it was simply a problem with his breathing that had grown worse.

That August a statue of the Blessed Mother was brought to San Giovanni from Fatima, the city in Portugal where Mary had appeared to three young children in 1917. Padre Pio had always loved Mary in a special way, so he had himself carried to the church where the statue was on display. After he finished praying in front of the statue, he had himself carried home.

Then, the day that the statue was being taken back to Portugal, he told the Blessed Virgin Mary that as long as she (her statue) had been in Italy, he had been ill. He asked that his illness might be carried away when she left. The very minute that the statue was taken away, Padre Pio jumped up out of bed and proclaimed that he had been healed.

Padre Pio Dies on the Fiftieth Anniversary of Receiving the Stigmata

BY 1968 many of Padre Pio's friends and disciples had died. He himself had grown quite weak, and one of the friars kept watch on him day and night in case he needed someone's help. He had difficulty sleeping and could barely walk. He often asked Padre Carmelo, his guardian, for permission to die.

Then, on September 20, 1968, the community and people from all over the world gathered in San Giovanni to celebrate the fiftieth anniversary of Padre Pio's reception of the stigmata. This was also the First International Convention of Padre Pio Prayer Groups.

Padre Pio celebrated Mass that morning, and he was able to be present when the people recited the Rosary and prayed in front of the Blessed Sacrament.

But by the next morning, he was so weak again that he could neither listen to confessions nor celebrate Mass. On September 22 he did celebrate Mass once again, but he was clearly quite ill. Late that night his condition grew worse, and he asked one of the friars to listen to his confession. He gave his last blessing to his spiritual disciples and uttered his last words: "Jesus and Mary." At 2:30 that morning Padre Pio died peacefully.

Padre Pio Is Beatified and Canonized

SO many people believed that Padre Pio was a Saint that by the next year the Capuchin friars had asked the Church to consider making him a Saint. Over the next several years all of his writings and actions were examined, and by 1983 the official process for his beatification had begun.

He was named Blessed on May 2, 1999. Then, on June 16, 2002, Pope John Paul II declared Padre Pio to be a Saint. His feast day is celebrated on September 23, and to this day many people pray for his intercession and speak of the favors they have received from God through him.